FURTHER

Also by Joy Howard

From Grey Hen Press
SECOND BITE
(with Hilary J Murray and Gina Shaw)
EXIT MOONSHINE

Edited by Joy Howard from Grey Hen Press

A TWIST OF MALICE
CRACKING ON
NO SPACE BUT THEIR OWN
GET ME OUT OF HERE!
THE PRICE OF GOLD
RUNNING BEFORE THE WIND
TRANSITIONS
OUTLOOK VARIABLE
SHADES OF MEANING
EXTRAORDINARY FORMS
SONGS FOR THE UNSUNG
VASTER THAN EMPIRES

From Ward Wood Publishing
REFURBISHMENT
From Arachne Press
FORAGING

FURTHER THAN IT LOOKS

Poems about mountains

Edited by Joy Howard

First published in 2019 by Grey Hen Press
PO Box 269
Kendal
Cumbria
LA9 9FE
www.greyhenpress.com

ISBN   978-0-9933756-9-9

Printed by Flexpress, Birstall, Leicester LE4 3BY

*With thanks to Annie Duckworth for her inspiring
knowledge and love of mountains*

THE THREE RULES OF MOUNTAINEERING

It's always further than it looks.
It's always taller than it looks.
And it's always harder than it looks.

Author Unknown

Contents

People

Introduction

Summit

You are not in the mountains. The mountains are in you.
John Muir

I need no wings
your rock has guided
me into sky

birds fly
below me
clouds drifts by

wind whispers
in the small hollow
my back is warm

feet regret
each downward step
this cleaving.

Fiona Ritchie Walker

Terrain

Volcanology

Black Coombe is silent now,
squatting at the top of Morecambe Bay,
the clouds around the summit not smoke,

only mist and unrelenting rain.
No one walking there has ever claimed
to have felt the faintest trembling

in grey slate far below their feet
or sensed a slight vibration in the air.
Still, I like to think some fissure exists,

a fistula tracking back to the earth's hot heart;
that without due notice given,
no plume, no sound, no sulphurous stink,

the mountain will erupt and pyroclastic flow
swallow the island. It's close,
a few miles north, but there'll be time enough,

I know, to say one thing. And I want
to give myself over to it, to let go,
to watch my name evaporate, to blaze.

Kate Davis

Landslip
Mynydd Carn y Cefn

It appeared suddenly, a quick rip in silk;
a green shirt tearing so as to expose
an unexpected piece of underneath.

A backscar, marking the length of a new slip,
the next instalment in the slow collapse
of the mountain on whose knee my house sits.

Over the years custodians have abused it,
piling detritus from their greedy beavering
shoulder-high into its long, green lap.

This was no way to treat so young a mountain.
In a few millennia its baby shales
might have matured and hardened into slate.

They worked it too hard, like a chimney sweep,
stealing its youth and dirtying its beauty;
scrambling its soft insides, breaking its bones.

They've tried to make amends, to kiss it better
by carting off the spoil and planting trees
but still the ground shifts and the cracks appear.

There is an outside chance the lot may go
and there is a Procedure written down
but nobody will tell me what it is.

Someone let slip that such a thing exists
and I was suddenly afraid, wondering –
if it happens, what will descend on us?

First the brown envelopes to The Occupier.
Clipboards, Confusion. Rows of pens in pockets.
I've got a job to do, love. Don't ask me!

Power of small men in big situations.
Ordering. Hectoring. Nobody listening.
Hopelessness. Impotence. Authority.

I was afraid; not of the changing face
of the mountain, but the unbending aspect
of a few little people in the valley.

Time has eroded the rough edge of terror.
The mountain smiles as the sun warms its corners
and shifts imperceptibly in its sleep.

But I still play *what I would do if the mountain fell*
because I am the sort of person I am
and because, sooner or later, the mountain will.

Ann Drysdale

Old Friend

I've known you
since I was a child
watched you
as soon as I could walk
or ride
to Birkrigg
gazed at you
from the Common

know the silhouette
of your body etched
against northern sky.

Even far from home I know you

know the dryness of you in winter
can see, now, drops of ice, hanging
from bent leaves of grass
scent of peat and sheep dung, look up
see the slow dance of ravens
above your shoulder; turn round

to Harter fell and Seathwaite
recall the long walk home down
the Duddon Valley one spring
banks peppered with wild daffodils.

I know the sharp ridge of your crags
and pikes, the way you dip,
gently, into Goat's Hause
only to rise up along the long flank
to your summit

where, in later life, I'd stand
look back
across the Bay and time
to rolling moors
pick out Hoad and Birkrigg
from the Alt Maen of Coniston
companions: Dow Crag
Brown Pike, Buck.

Geraldine Green

Caer Bran

Sky

the wide bowl
and being up in it   in the scoured air
out of the moist woods

Green wears camouflage colours
dun   sage   pewter   beige
bush and stone sharing a palette

Gorse and bracken clump   push in
on squeezed paths

What remains of rampart
is still on guard

White butterfly wearing a trellis of grey
settles on a slab   moves on

This is wind's country
never off duty   it chases lassitude
back down the contour
to the valleys

You are waiting for me
at home here in this high place
of the protector

All horizon   land falling away
until it topples into haze
beyond is what we have left behind

We walk the rim   sound the bowl of sky.

Jennie Osborne

Great Gable

Such hopes

of splendour:

but now the path is gone

storm clouds are blowing in

the mountain losing

height and majesty

has become

just a few square metres

of hail-strafed enemy territory

under a low sky   spitting

bitter rain.

Joy Howard

On Kinder

Here those giants
Nature and Weather
laboured for aeons
with threadless needles
in and out of
the moving picture.

Are labouring still
as we stand in the wind
and it sews us in
with tussock and cloud
and the Downfall's spray.

With feather and moss
briar and fern
master-embroiderers
stitch the day

Frances Nagle

Causey Pike from Derwentwater

Foothills like ginger cake:
dun-brown and straight-topped.
A pale track snakes up
diagonally to the next tier
where a dusting of icing sugar
reveals the covert terracettes
in faint layers upon the slope.

If I were to climb, I'd need
crampons, wind-proofs,
and guts for the summit.
But from here I can enjoy
the raised scar, curving
proud round the top,
its ugly knotted seam
outstanding in the snow.

Hilary Tattershall

Snaefell in Snow

No cars passed from Creg Na Baa that month
so thick the blizzards. No motorbikes screeched

round its corner, no one died, except the sheep,
lost and buried in the fields. One flock, moved

indoors, crushed in the farmer's barn when snow
collapsed the roof. The road to Snaefell peak,

snow-hedged, six feet high, led silently where
sun diffused its slow-paced thaw, white shapes

spread outwards on the grasses, melted inwards
on themselves. Icy leprous limbs lay shrunk

beside their torso-walls, and all the time
our footprints sank down inches to compacted ice.

On distant hillsides, pale scars criss-crossed
down the slopes, framed by pure white boulders,

Fheaps fashioned by machines and men from
days before, which dug to clear and dug to find.

The railway frozen, carriages abandoned,
two thousand feet flowed into quiet stretch.

Jane Monach

MacGillicuddy's Reeks
(na cruacha dubha)

the black stacks have snatched
the snow out of the sky
leaving only scatterings for the fields

the reeks are smug in their glory
show new folds and facets
corral climbers and sheep to the foothills

the peaks are closer but more remote
life scuttles under the white mask
soon colour will spear through the melt

Jennifer Russell

She Mountain

Eyjafjallajoekull remembers the kind of place she is;
Her personality split at the start of time.
The rock just a bed to sleep in for unpredictable spells,
until her dreams involving us are done and she turns
with fitful gasps of waking into this revision.
Her ice, no longer innocent, becomes a vast machinery.
She thunders as she breaks it and the plates of rock
beneath her, for she is proud and terrible as she ruptures.

She's a body with a core of hell and lightning,
made up of an old testament she herself invented
in her long and gaseous slumber. Now she flies,
oh how she flies, awesome and most ravishing.
Her mouth pulses ignition red, her lips smoulder black
and the massive white of her risen dress is everywhere.

Susan Taylor

On Mount Etna

The sun is bright but does not warm.
Snow, clouds, drifting plumes,
lava, steaming fumaroles.
I sit suspended in thin air
alone in silent monochrome.
My senses thrum in vacuum,
my ears vibrating for a sound.

No bird, no tree, no blade of grass.
No houses, cars or barking dogs.
No breeze. Above, a deep blue sky;
below, the land spread out like sea.
Sullen brimstone. Then I hear
a butterfly battling its yellow wings
across the barren heights.

Anne Boileau

Pigeon House Mountain

We climb past mountain ash and wattle,
through the wet forest with its lyrebirds.

The aborigines named the mountain Didthol,
their word for a woman's breast

and these days you can scale the nipple
on vertical ladders, not looking down,

though, if you did, you'd see all the way
from Point Perpendicular to Mount Dromedary.

I prefer the rocks under my feet and the old words,
Ulladulla, Byangee, Croobyar, Budawang.

Carole Bromley

Mottarone

Mountains amassed like a herd

of bulls, their nostrils

emitting puffs of smoke,

horns snow white

hooking the sky's cloak.

Mottarone's a huge

cow in their midst,

placid, ruminating;

rocks in the meadows

milking stools.

Gabriel Griffin

Mynydd Llangatwg

There's a mountain in my window
each morning when I wake up
there it is   dimmed with mist or sharp -
sun-cast into gloom or blanked out
by rain. Long and low, no peak
but a rounded crown, as if a standing giant
were buried to the top of his skull.

It looks massive, but is just a shell
over empty space
hollowed out by water: great caves,
warrens, squeezes of limestone
where little humans wriggle through
like an infestation.

It looks immutable; but men
have gouged long galleries
below the dome till it looks
like a stormtrooper's helmet.
The quarrymen are long gone.
The clawmarks will not heal.

It looks eternal; but it's not long
since its Ice Age birth. Time,
water, weather, men have worked it. Time
will wear it away utterly, and if by then
Valleys people and posh people still exist
they won't need to go over the top
to see one another's faces.

Maybe someday, though, long after
the houses in between have collapsed
and returned to woodland
so long that even the plastic roof-tiles
will have perished
as though they had never been, time
might throw up a new mountain.

Stevie Krayer

Through the Boxroom Window
(Divis, near Belfast)

paving slabs
flat, shining
under the street lights
lead the eye upwards

to where
a blue-black sky
drenches
a blue-black mountain

blackens it, blackens
it more—

how can this
squat, quarried
mass at the edge
of a city ringed
with fear
and boredom

(evening air damp
and sweet, pungent
with coal smoke)

how can this
be a thing I
can't breathe
without?

Nora Hughes

Mount Monadnock

The only fault I find with old New Hampshire
Is that her mountains aren't quite high enough.

Robert Frost

When we first met
how thin I was, all elbows
and knees, and you granite

and spruce, hemlock, bristling,
not soaring, sharing the same hours
and light with me.

Probably I was aware of you
in the corner of my eye – there,
reassuring, but no more than that.

Now you mean to be looked at
even at night, or from this faraway
time zone. When ice lays hold of you

and snow, I can crawl along your granite,
eye to eye with you, and feel fear
and a modest ambition.

Yet for me, dark or light,
these days it's all a matter of touch –
from your hand a single leaf

or even a pine needle would do.

Jane Duran

Cader Idris

When the stars are occluded
by cold fits of rain

when the rockrose of the heart
presses through pain

to burst a red bud
by the bone's white thorn

then still you are there
dreaming falcons, ethers,

light on the wing, your slate-grey
mantle lifting

through haze. Massed
against the sky's uncertainties.

Lynne Wycherley

People

Ridge Walking

This
is my life
out here
on this edge.

Windy here
– a narrow ridge.

Often I am scared,
have to squeeze my eyes shut,
hug myself to the rock,
crawl along on all fours
mumbling mantras.

But sometimes
I dance the thin line,
whirling in the sun,
shouting in an arms-up,
head-back laugh.

This
is my life out here.
A slim chance
with steep drops on either side,
but the views
are bloody marvellous.

Char March

Killing Me Softly

First stop in sunshine, low July sky not yet
leaking rain, overlooks
Llyn Llydaw's agate splash, set
in a green fold outspread below.
Now the rocks are seeping drizzle,
Soon, my stick's a handicap, stabbing at stone
as if I'm blind in alien territory,
catching in cracks, useless on slippery slate.
No help for awkward grandmother's feet.
My hands are levers, hauling up the too big slabs.
This onslaught on Snowdon's ancient tuffs
is taking its toll. Slowed to the rear, I'm told
to keep a straighter path, but age, not choice
dictates my straying. Lungs complain,
calves unpractised for too long aren't happy.
I snatch a breath, and see the view has vanished.
Six yards distant, mist has blanked out all.
Yr Wyddfa's age-old trick, cheating the invaders
with a sly, veiled face. This for all my toil.

Two thirds up, the second stop's too short
to ease the rougher track to come,hard
clambering for fragile bones, with holds
precarious as these edges. Ahead, figures shrink
melt and disappear amidst black crags, or loom
on downward trek. The scene is monochrome.
Urged on, I'm frogmarched between guides
to mount the cafe steps, squeezing through crowds
for respite, last sandwich and a seat. It's enough.
Descending by the miners track, I crunch
beside the leader. Straight off the grey pall lifts,
shifts towards the summit. Pewter and emerald
unroll to Llanberis, flanks of boulder, shale
and pebble washed to brilliance. The valley
fills with light, features sharp in focus.
This then is my epiphany. Why I loved you,
casting your spell so many years ago.

Rosemary Doman

Uphill

When we embarked
on the steep incline
earlier this morning,
it was encouraging to see
the brow quite clearly

but as we climbed
towards where it had first
appeared to be, our goal
receded, keeping nearly half
an upward mile further on

after an hour of trudging
into wind, the ground
started to descend,
but only for a few short
quickened steps

before it rose again:
our hard-won hill top
clearly just a milestone
on the way to
greater heights

Alwyn Marriage

Epiphany

I chose this route, the shorter, harder climb,
not guessing how terrain would change
from rock-strewn path to sheer,
fist-gripping, nail-tearing slate.

Others strained beside me, overtook,
muscles ribbed with taut veins,
faces clenched and weathered.

It was a relief to realise
they had clambered out of sight,
left me hauling breath
into laboured lungs.
I reached a ledge,
rested, my back sloped in stone,
dared to look down.

And from that point it seemed
my gaze could trace
lines of land
that contorted into its contours,
forests where dinosaurs lumbered,
the how and why of grass.

I met the others at the summit,
panted until pulses slowed,
shared thermos-stewed tea.

I never told them
how my vision had shifted,
that I knew the answers
for one bright nanosecond.

We took the longer, gentler path down;
talked of football and the price of fish.

Alison Chisholm

Reckoning

Each foot taking us
faster-slow, shadows
before the range
we angled towards it.
Beyond the scattered
settlements, our paths
spanned out.

Soon we hiked by
waterfalls;
our tracks zigzagged
the mountain's furred skin.
This was like work:
the weight and sweat
of the climb
pulling us back
in our push towards
that line
far away enough
to meet the sky.

Stepping over bramble
we urged each other forward,
leaving everything we knew
behind. The mountain
owned us. Our faces
wore together
like two sides of a coin.

Katherine Gallagher

The Question
Old Halterburnhead, Pennine Way

This is the gate,
And this the hill. Low sun lays bare the mile
On mile of folded fell, gold ridge and hollow.

It is easy to be lost.
You tease the passing walkers – 'Are we right for Byrness?' –
Though it's a hard day's hike away, and getting late,

As you well know.

So we arrive at the tree-line; sycamores,
A ruined shiel among blackened nettles,
Deep in the cleugh, a burn, quickthorn, a fallen sheep-stell;

So many endeavours –
Stone dyke, lichenous boulder, earthwork – leading back
Into the misty blue of a far distant past

Or future. Now

We are sprawled full length on the spring grass, body to body,
Clover leaf, sheep dung, under us, under our kisses.
What I most want on earth presses upon us.

It is not huge, the question. It is weightless,
A skylark, doodling above us, a swallow
Vanishing into the blue. There is only one answer.

My word was No.

How could it have been otherwise? How
Can anything ever be otherwise – though every day
For the rest of my life I shall ask it: How

Could I not have known, could I not have known – on the green fell,
Under miles of sky, by the gate we did not go through,
The hills stretching on and on, untrodden, into nightfall?

Katrina Porteous

Snowdon

In that spring of raw love
we rushed on to the Pyg Track
from the steamy cafe of Pen-y-Pass.

Riding the spine of rough peaks,
following the track where miners carried black tar,
we stumbled into knee-deep, soggy snow.

Laughing, you dragged me ever higher,
my hair a smudge of soft brown,
your hand warm as a bird's breast.

I have a photograph of us
perched above a muscular stream
whose water turned fingers to ice.

I'm open as a cat's yawn,
bare faced as the rocks piled around us
who had seen it all before:

the arduous climb, short breaths
coming fast in clouds of mist,
the slippery, treacherous descent.

The *afanc* monster coiled on the river bed
roared so loud I heard nothing you said.
Later I left you. Of course I did.

Caroline Gilfillan

Y Berwyn
for Jacqueline Glasser

The setting sun
cuts the flank

of the bare mountain
in two,

the top half
gladdened

by rose-red molten light,
the lower half

dark-blue scree
and parched heather,

no-man's land of dusk

Driving the high mountain pass
we find the last of the light

The road can go
no higher

nor can the light
be less than the one true thing

Sheep disdain
our top-speed presence

and so do
the peaks and valleys –

we dash along
our tightrope of light

as it keeps
its rocky nerve

These heights
are the bright lit places

no one dares to doubt
and when the sun slips down

the far side of the gulley
that dimming

is another kind of brilliance,
inward and implicate,

as the road descends
and the mountains forget us

Penelope Shuttle

Heading for the Heights

Why did she seek out the mountains?
January, force nines yelling,
the black bog, minimal tracks rained out,
the waterfall, iced solid.

When all sane people were boarded up,
not daring to venture far from
their hot pipes, when her children called –
why need she go? What drove her?

The same, perhaps, that drives me from
the car-infested valleys
to climb, till only the ancient pack-roads
are left, on top of the world.

You see them, heading for the heights,
on most mornings this winter,
equipped, you think, for the long haul –
maps, snow-boots and compass.

Wander all night. Doctors and missionaries
untraced, lone farms inaccessible;
how easy, on the calmest day,
to lose your track and perish.

Each year, the bodies lie unclaimed,
and some, never discovered.
Yet still they head for the high ground,
no child's crying will stop them.

Merryn Williams

The Black Cuillin

What fatal error undermined your skill,
when you set off without a glance behind,
upon the slopes of those forbidding hills.

Escaping to the mountains and their thrill,
with trusted friends you knew to be your kind,
what fatal error undermined your skill.

You ventured out alone to breathe your fill,
a short walk in the sunshine to unwind,
upon the slopes of those forbidding hills.

The sea lay tranquil and the island still.
I wonder if their magic made you blind,
as hidden peril undermined your skill.

No one was there to see you fall and spill
your youth and all the plans you had in mind,
upon the slopes of those forbidding hills.

The Black Cuillin captured your free will,
and shrouds the jagged facts so we can't find
what fatal error undermined your skill,
upon the slopes of those forbidding hills.

Frances White

Highest Mountain

In my blue-and-white bathroom
the blue-and-white picture. Up close
you faintly see the folds
made on its long journey:
Lukla, Kathmandu, Doha, Heathrow, Teesside.

You might say I never arrived
never touched the mountain or set foot
on it. Never risked life for it
though there was payment of pain:
thighs, calves, feet suffered

on those giant stairways of rock,
day after day approaching.
Then at last we saw it.
'Straight ahead,' the guide said. Invisible.
But the white curtain slid back

soundlessly and there it was,
a smoke of snow-crystals rising.
No camera to come between us.
Its likeness in my eyes
its ice-breath on my skin.

My picture reminds me.
The summit towering godlike.
White peak with its blue shadows
as if it stood so high
the sky was seeping in.

Chris Considine

St. Elias Range, Yukon Territory

snow crunches underfoot
ice-crystals spring apart   change their nature
as we make our way
one boot at a time
each one in front of the last one
       precise
       as tightrope walkers
treading uninterrupted whiteness
falling away on both sides
so steep   pebble-like balls of snow
dislodged by our boots
fly into gasps of air
thin air   *ha ha*
everything's thin   at this altitude
even the mind stomps along
only half there   on the knife-edge ridge
but the crest's ahead
           the solidity
of jutting rock
a kiss from the handsome guide
and that monarch-of-the-world headiness
of a view seen only
by helicopters hawks and eagles
       perhaps pain's always needed
pain   fear of heights   infatuation with everything

I laughed when
armed with ice-axe and crampons
we retraced our steps so easily
down a 100 foot wall
easy breath returning
       back on level ground
all had seemed good   very good

until the exhaustion ahead
a seven-mile walk
through the woods

I was the last one back to camp
on hands and knees
expecting to be eaten
by the resident grizzly bear
     in the idiotic way
     one's mind works at altitude
     I spoke to him   *please don't eat my feet*
     they were so great on the mountain

Caroline Carver

Looking for the Cuillins

Not Skye, you say, sure to rain
been that way six times
and all I've seen of the Cuillin
a rumour in the mist

But I persuade you in sunshine
that holds to Kintail — then cloud
turns drizzle turns rain, a mean rain
that crescendoes to deluge
at Kyleakin

The kind of rain
that makes heroes of wipers
doesn't halt for breath
through three dark days
and nights

I show you (from the car)
Sgathach's place in Sleat
you say she deserves
her Warrior Queen title
                just
for weathering Skye
weather

So no mountains again …

But in the hotel bar
you're quick to see
Red Cuillin and Black Cuillin
beers galore

And they cost me!

But Slàinte
Slàinte, my friend
for not saying
not even once
I told you so

Maggie Rabatski

Father Mountain

Mount Baker soars whiteclad above the clouds
across the Strait, hovering like a mirage,
like an angel, over Victoria, its wings
sheltering the lower range it towers above.
More often, these peaks are hidden in the haze,
and only the higher slopes,
shimmering from seventy miles away,
reveal themselves, floating, weightless,
in the blue arch of sky.

My mother made her pilgrimage each day,
as Hokusai paid his tribute to Mount Fuji;
her devotion as nebulous as the vision
of this peak, conveyed not through tangible
offerings of art, but through the palpable
delight of mindful daily observation.
It was as if her father, a volcanologist,
held her always in his loving watch, through
the long difficult days of her old age.

Rosemary McLeish

Preseli

Zig-zag we leapt reed island to tuft
and under us the wind flashed the pools.
Then nervous sheep lurched up to plod away
and fog-rags swam the cairns of Foeldrygarn.

The horizon rose like a pockmarked moon.

In rain Beddarthur stones woke up
and trod their place.
We saw a listening ring.
Sharpened our wits, stepped in.

Jean Atkin

Dawn

Keep still and the birds will forget you are there
Nan Shepherd

On this mountain of winter veil, home
to cudweed, saxifrage and fern – those
who wake beyond bracken and whin,

a deer reveals its bursting heart traversing
slate-edged screes to feed on a fold of juniper
and yew creviced in rock. I watch light begin

to soften muscle, sharpen edges, trails
and marsh lost to those who don't know
the harsh distance of Herdwicks' hefted graze,

I travel without movement, quiescence
of no human steps, violet haze, warm breath
descending these autonomous crags.

Kerry Darbishire

The Fell Ponies

They would raise their heads if I called, and stare
and begin to jostle friendly or unfriendly
from the country of no words, seeming
to crave the human; and I'd push the hair
from flat foreheads and peaty eyes and offer
pieces of bread, till the stallion squealed.

Then I knew them cousin to the Centaurs
who shouldered in eager and shy to the wedding
of the Lapiths and tasted their drink
and grew mad with the strangeness, rioting,
bursting the palisades.

                  Wastes, islands of heather,
green mosses where the ponies drifted
among pools as acid as spoiled wine:
I'd go there once, guest without invitation
at the high weddings of earth and air.

M R Peacocke

The Blue Hill - Cairngorm

Wild and beautiful, the high blue hill,
a granite plateau scored with glens and corries;
winter snowfields mantle its soft mosses,
and at the melting margins dotterels find
rich insect harvests, rare snow-bunting nest;
cloudberry, dwarf birch and least willow
make their home here; starry saxifrage,
twin-flower and moss campion rejoice
in their small out-post of sub-arctic tundra.
Wild and beautiful the blue hill, fragile too,
exposed to the smallest interferences
of man and beast and climate.

Love also has its own ecology,
intimate and delicately balanced:
it too is a lifelong study, needing patience
and stewardship, like any living system.
The balance shifts, the sun shines fitfully,
shadows race across the changing landscape.
We should be respectful guardians
of our own high blue hill, learn to wear
lightly its loveliness and singularity,
in snowfall or rainfall, sun-fall or leaf-fall,
secure always in the underlying
steadfastness of granite.

Elisabeth Rowe

Biographical Notes

Jean Atkin's new collection *How Time is in Fields* was published by IDP in 2019. She is a poet working in education and community projects. *Anne Boileau* lives in Essex. Her novel *Katharina Luther* was published in 2016 and her new poetry collection *Dreams of Flight* is due out later this year. *Carole Bromley* lives in York. She has three collections with Smith/Doorstop and is an Arvon tutor and mentor for the Poetry Society. *Caroline Carver* was a mountaineer and rock climber when she lived in Canada. These days she's a poet – perhaps the same thing. *Alison Chisholm* is a poetry tutor and adjudicator, and the author of eleven collections. She writes poetry columns for 'Writing Magazine', and textbooks on the craft of writing poetry. *Chris Considine* now lives in Devon, having left Yorkshire. Her fifth collection, Seeing Eye, has recently been published by Cinnamon Press *Kerry Darbishire* is widely published in anthologies and journals. Collections: *A Lift of Wings* and *Distance Sweet on my Tongue* (Indigo Dreams). Biography: *Kay's Ark* (Handstand Press). *Kate Davis* is from Barrow-in-Furness. Her poems have been implanted in audio-benches, sung, remixed and printed on bags. Her first collection is *The Girl Who Forgets How to Walk.* *Rosemary Doman* is a former Creative Writing tutor who has been published in a number of anthologies and won prizes for several of her poems. *Ann Drysdale* is an English poet living in Wales on the lower slopes of the mountain of which she writes. *Jane Duran* was born in Cuba and raised in the USA and Chile. She lives in London and has published five poetry collections with Enitharmon Press. *Katherine Gallagher* is Australian-born and London-based. She is a poetry tutor and writes for adults and children. She has has six collections. *Caroline Gilfillan* has published four poetry collections. Her first novel, *The Terrace*, came out in 2018. *Geraldine Green,* writer-in-residence at The Quaker Tapestry Museum Kendal, has a PhD in Creative Writing from Lancaster University. New collection: *Passing Through* (Indigo Dreams). *Gabriel Griffin* Founder (2001)/organiser of *Poetry on the Lake* annual competition & events on Lake Orta; published in anthologies and journals. *Joy Howard* lives in Cumbria among beautiful and much loved mountains, sadly now inaccessible to a largely sedentary woman in her late seventies. *Nora Hughes* grew up in Belfast and now lives in London. Her poems have appeared in anthologies and magazines, most recently in *Envoi* and *The North*. *Stevie Krayer's* publications include three poetry collections, a translation of Rilke's *The Book of Hours* and an anthology of Quaker poets, *A Speaking Silence* (with R V Bailey). **Rosemary McLeish**, Scottish artist and poet, now lives in Kent. *I Am a Field*, her first full collection, is just out from Wordsmithery. **Char March** is an award-winning poet and playwright. Her fifth poetry collection is 'Full Stops in Winter Branches' (Valley Press).**Alwyn Marriage** 's ten published books include poetry, fiction and non-fiction. She is Managing Editor of Oversteps Books and research fellow at Surrey University. **Jane Monach** worked in mentalhealth and education; now lives in Sheffield where she writes, and explores poetry with a number of groups. **Frances Nagle** is enjoying her golden years reading, writing, exploring the hidden corners of Italy and indulging grandchildren. **Jennie Osborne** is one of the organisers of Teignmouth Poetry Festival. Two collections from Oversteps, latest 'Colouring Outside the Lines'. **Meg Peacocke** The memory of wild places gives me continued life. I am lucky to have known them. **Katrina Porteous** was born in Scotland and lives in Northumberland. Her third collection with Bloodaxe is due out later this year.**Maggie Rabatski** is currently working with AC Clarke and Sheila Templeton on a second poetry pamphlet in the three languages of Scotland, to follow *Owersettin'* (Tapsalteerie) published in 2016. **Elisabeth Rowe** 's fourth collection will be published by Oversteps Books in 2019. She continues to write in both serious and comic vein. **Jennifer Russell** lives in the south-west of Ireland. She has recently published her first chapbook with Grey Hen Press. **Penelope Shuttle's** latest collection *Will You Walk A Little Faster?* was published by Bloodaxe Books in 2017. She is President of The Falmouth Poetry Group. **Hilary Tattershall** has lived in Cockermouth for thirteen years. After retiring she rediscovered creativity: she now writes, sews and draws. **Susan Taylor** is a former shepherd, turned wolf enthusiast. She has seven published collections – the first dating back to 1977. **Fiona Ritchie Walker** regularly volunteers on National Trust for Scotland work camps. Her poem began in a soggy notebook while walking in Wester Ross. **Frances White** sadly died of Motor Neurone Disease before the publication of this book. She was widely published during her lifetime, and her collection, *Swiftscape,* won high praise. **Merryn Williams** ' latest collection is *The Fragile Bridge: New and Selected Poems* (Shoestring Press). Her poem was inspired by Alison Hargreaves. **Lynne Wycherley's** latest book *Testimony of the Trees* (Shoestring 2018) is a prayer for the living world in the face of digital excesses. She lives in Devon.

Acknowledgements

JEAN ATKINS 'Preseli' published in *Coast to Coast to Coast* 2018;
CAROL BROMLEY 'Pigeon House Mountain' *The Stonegate Devil*
Smith/Doorstop, 2015; ALISON CHISHOLM 'Epiphany' *A
Fraction from Parallel* Caleta Publishing 2016. KATE DAVIS 'Vul-
canology' *The Girl Who Forgets How to Walk* Penned in the Margins
2018; ANN DRYSDALE 'Landslip' *Backwork* Peterloo Poets 2002;
JANE DURAN 'Mount Monadnock' *American Sampler* Enith-
armon Press 2014; KATHERINE GALLAGHER 'Reckoning'
Carnival Edge: New & Selected Poems Arc Publications 2010; NORA
HUGHES 'Through the Boxroom Window' published in Envoi
2019; CHAR MARCH 'Ridge Walking' *The Thousand Natural
Shocks* Indigo Dreams 2011; ALWYN MARRIAGE 'Uphill'
Welcome to the Hills Ledbury website 2018; FRANCES NAGLE
'On Kinder' *Derbyshire* Poet's England, Headland 2000 and *The
War in Fraxius Excelsior* Dagger Press 2001; M R PEACOCKE 'The
'Fell Ponies' *Caliban Dancing* Shoestring 2011; SUSAN TAYLOR
'She Mountain' *Temporal Bones* Oversteps Books 2016; FRANCES
WHITE 'The Black Cuillin' *Swiftscape* The Seventh Quarry Press
2016; MERRYN WILLIAMS 'Heading for the Heights' *The Sun's
Yellow Eye* National Poetry Foundation 1997.

Joy Howard is the founder of Grey Hen Press, which specialises in publishing the work of older women poets. Her poems have featured in many anthologies and journals and can be found online at *poetry p f.* She has edited thirteen previous Grey Hen Press anthologies, and published a collection of her own poems *Exit Moonshine* about her 'coming out' experiences in the 1980s. Her second collection, *Refurbishment,* was published by Ward Wood in 2011, and her most recent, *Foraging,* by Arachne Press in 2016.